Assessing the Personal Financial Problems of Junior Enlisted Personnel

Richard Buddin

D. Phuong Do

Prepared for the
Office of the Secretary of Defense

National Defense Research Institute

RAND

The research described in this report was sponsored by the Office of the Secretary of Defense (OSD). The research was conducted in RAND's National Defense Research Institute, a federally funded research and development center supported by the OSD, the Joint Staff, the unified commands, and the defense agencies under Contract DASW01-95-C-0059.

Library of Congress Cataloging-in-Publication Data

Buddin, Richard J., 1951–
    Assessing the personal financial problems of junior enlisted personnel / Richard Buddin, D. Phuong Do.
      p. cm.
    "MR-1444."
    Includes bibliographical references.
    ISBN 0-8330-3164-3
    1. Soldiers—United States—Finance, Personal. 2. United States—Armed Forces—Pay, allowances, etc. 3. Sailors—Uniteds States—Finance, Personal. I. Do, D. Phuong. II.Title.

UC74 .B844 2002
355.3'4—dc21

                                   2002021396

Published 2002 by RAND
1700 Main Street, P.O. Box 2138, Santa Monica, CA 90407-2138
1200 South Hayes Street, Arlington, VA 22202-5050
201 North Craig Street, Suite 102, Pittsburgh, PA 15213
RAND URL: http://www.rand.org/
To order RAND documents or to obtain additional information,
contact Distribution Services: Telephone: (310) 451-7002;
Fax: (310) 451-6915; Email: order@rand.org

PREFACE

This research examines the extent and nature of personal financial management problems for junior enlisted personnel. These problems are widespread and consume substantial amounts of military management time. The problems place stress on military members that may adversely affect their job performance and diminish the quality of life for them and their families. The military has traditionally taken an active role in addressing personnel financial problems through classes and counseling. These efforts have intensified in recent years, but member problems remain numerous.

The Deputy Assistant Secretary of Defense for Military Community and Family Policy sponsored the research. This research should interest those concerned with military families, the well-being of servicemembers, the attendant implications for recruiting and retention, and the relationship between military and civilian communities.

The research was conducted in the Forces and Resources Policy Center, which is part of RAND's National Defense Research Institute, a federally funded research and development center sponsored by the Office of the Secretary of Defense, the Joint Staff, the unified commands, and the defense agencies.

CONTENTS

FIGURES

TABLES

SUMMARY

BACKGROUND AND PURPOSE

Military life subjects servicemembers and their families to a variety of stresses. These include unexpected deployments, long separations, and isolation from parents and other family members, to name a few. The military services are interested in reducing the source and intensity of the stress affecting their members. Surveys of military personnel show that, particularly for junior personnel, financial problems constitute a major source of stress, subordinate only to increased workload and family separation.

The services have a vested interest in reducing the number and type of financial problems their members have because they not only have a negative effect on individual family well-being, but they also can lead to poor job performance. Thus, determining the nature and extent of the financial problems afflicting military personnel and whether these problems differ substantially in type and number from comparable members of civilian society could provide policymakers with important information. At the request of the Department of Defense, the National Defense Research Institute conducted a study to answer these questions.

SOURCE AND NATURE OF OUR DATA

For the military population, we drew our data from two types of sources. One was a series of visits to military installations, where we conducted focus groups in which we queried a range of personnel about the financial problems experienced by junior enlisted military members, defined here as those with less than 10 years of service. We also had access to two random-sample surveys that included demographic as well as financial information.

Our data about the civilian population derives from a longitudinal study that has been conducted since 1968. We used data from the 1996 survey and excluded data for civilians who were over 40 or were full-time students so that we had a population that compared well with the military members.

WHAT WE FOUND OUT

The results of our research group into three areas:

- The nature and number of financial problems junior enlisted have.

- How their problems compare with a similar civilian population.

- The effect of unique aspects of military life on financial problems.

Nature and Number of Problems

The results show that a substantial fraction of the junior enlisted force has financial problems and that the members are aware of their problems. Subjective measures on a self-reported survey show that about 20 percent of junior enlisted personnel struggle to make ends meet financially and another 4 percent regard themselves as "in over their heads." The objective measures of specific bill problems (e.g., individual was pressured by creditors to pay bills, had utilities shut off, or pawned valuables to pay debts) paint a similar picture. They show that 26 percent of the junior military members have serious problems paying bills. The Army and the Marine Corps have the most problems, and the Air Force has the fewest.

Across the services, the level of the problems has decreased. From 1997 to 1999, problems declined by about 5 percentage points. However, the reason for the decline remains unclear. All the services have educational programs to teach their members personal financial management. But the data do not enable us to determine if these programs are responsible for the decline or whether it results from other factors, such as an improved economy.

The problems do not seem to relate to family income. There appears to be no variation in the probability of having financial problems across the income range that accounts for 87 percent of the populations (less than $3,000 per month). Families with incomes above $3,000 a month are somewhat (6 percentage points) less likely to have a problem.

How the Junior Enlisted Force Compares with Civilians

The junior enlisted force has substantially more problems than does the comparable civilian population. An average of 20 percent of the military population reports being pressured by creditors compared with 10 percent of the civilian population. When it comes to paying bills, 27 percent of the military experiences problems compared with 19 percent of the comparable civilian group.

The two populations differ substantially in that the civilian populace is older, better educated, and has a more widely dispersed range of incomes. This comes as no surprise because the military recruits mostly young high school graduates, and almost 90 percent of them earn $3,000 a month or less. However, even after controlling for demographic and other characteristics, military personnel are substantially more likely to have financial problems than their civilian counterparts.

Demographic and family factors affect both groups in the same way. Problems with creditor pressure and paying bills both decline somewhat with age and more with education. Blacks have more problems than both Hispanics and white non-Hispanics.

There are also some differences. One difference appears in households headed by females. In the civilian populace, such households are 6 percentage points more likely to have financial problems than those headed by a male. In the military population, the likelihood of financial problems does not differ between those headed by males and females. Another difference appears in marital status. For each status, military members have more problems than do their civilian counterparts, but the patterns differ. Single and divorced civilians have the most problems, but in the military, singles have the lowest rate of problems.

Unique Aspects of Military Life

Some aspects of military life relate to having more financial problems, and some do not.

- Serious financial problems are 7 percentage points more common for married members separated from their families by a permanent change of station than for other members. The differential rises to 11 percentage points if the member has children.

- Long work hours are linked with financial difficulties: Bill problems are 3 percentage points higher for those working more than 50 hours per week than for those working shorter hours at their military job.

- Financial problems are more common for deployed members (more than one-month deployment in past year) than for members with no deployment history.

- Bill problems are 9 percentage points higher for members with a second job than for a comparable member who is not moonlighting in the civilian sector. This effect probably reflects members taking a second job because he or she has serious financial problems.

It does not appear to make a difference if a spouse has a full-time civilian job. When both the husband and wife are military members, the rate of serious financial problems is about 8 percentage points lower than for other comparable married members with a civilian spouse.

IMPLICATIONS

A key insight of this study is that two key factors are unrelated to financial distress for members. First, financial problems are not more common for members in off-base housing than for those living on base. Various reasons can justify expanding or contracting the stock of on-base housing, but our result suggests that these policies will have little effect on the extent of financial problems. Second, financial problems are not related to family income. Higher military pay would improve the well-being of members and their families, but our results suggest that the pay increase would do little to reduce the extent of financial problems among members. This finding suggests that financial problems are shaped by spending patterns and management skills rather than by the level of income.

We would encourage the Department of Defense (DoD) and the military services to implement a systematic evaluation of financial management programs. This evaluation would vary course offerings among members, test member financial skills before and after each type of training, and assess financial problems of members over time. This approach would identify which types of training are most effective and offer a clear path for reducing financial problems.

Our base visits did suggest two relatively untapped approaches that merit serious attention. First, unit officials provide considerable "hands-on" financial advice to young members, but these efforts are not well integrated with formal financial management classes. Too often, it appeared that unit leaders saw their efforts as alternatives to formal instruction and referred members to the formal programs as a last resort. We suspect that the personnel support managers could do a better outreach effort to advise unit leaders on how to "informally" help members. Second, the services should endeavor to reduce the stigma associated with financial counseling. Members are reluctant to use available services because they believe that they will be punished by the military for their financial situation. Similarly, some unit leaders are reluctant to recommend formal counseling for a member because they believe that a record of counseling will jeopardize the member's military future. One-on-one counseling could help members build a budget or arrange a consolidation loan, but the stigma of using the counseling services discourages members from taking advantage of these services.

ACKNOWLEDGMENTS

We are especially grateful to Iris Bulls and Linda Smith, formerly of the Office of the Deputy Assistant Secretary of Defense for Military Community and Family Policy, for their enthusiasm in initiating this study.

Among RAND colleagues, we are indebted to Susan Hosek, the former Director of the Forces and Resources Program, and Susan Everingham, the current director of the program, for their support and encouragement. We are grateful to Jerry Sollinger and Ron Zimmer for comments on an earlier draft. Eric Eide and Margaret Harrell provided valuable technical reviews of the report.

ACRONYMS

ADS	Active-Duty Survey (1999 DoD Survey of Military Personnel)
DoD	Department of Defense
ECI	Enlisted Career Intentions (1997 Survey of Junior Enlisted Personnel)
NCO	Noncommissioned officer
PCS	Permanent change of station
PSID	Panel Study of Income Dynamics (1996 Survey of Civilian Families)
SCF	Survey of Consumer Finance

Chapter One

INTRODUCTION

BACKGROUND

Many junior enlisted members of the military have difficulty managing their personal finances.[1] In a recent survey, about 15 percent of the members reported that having financial problems was a major source of stress in their lives (Bray et al., 1999). The only sources of stress greater than financial problems were time away from family (19.5 percent) and increases in workload (17.6 percent). Financial problems were a more widely perceived source of stress than many military-related factors, such as deployments, work situations, and military reassignments.

Financial problems affect the well-being of military members and their families, but the consequences of these problems may also affect job performance. Bray et al. (1999) found those members with high levels of stress had above-average incidences of problems with their military jobs (e.g., late for work, leaving work early, on-the-job injury, and below-normal performance). The study does not, however, establish a causal link between financial stress and job performance. Individuals with financial problems may have inherently lower productivity or be less motivated than other workers, and these factors may explain their lower productivity. For example, mildly depressed individuals will function poorly in both work and social settings, so they might have both reduced productivity and difficulties in paying bills. If the underlying problem is depression, teaching

---

[1]For the purposes of this study, we define junior enlisted members as enlisted personnel with 10 or less years of service.

financial management skills will do little to enhance individual workplace productivity.

In an earlier study (Tiemeyer et al., 1999), unit leaders and non-commissioned officers (NCOs) reported that financial problems were widespread for junior enlisted personnel. These problems consumed large amounts of member and management time. The financial problems frequently affected job performance directly as well as indirectly through fallout from subsequent family and marital problems.

In some severe cases, members are sent home during deployments to rectify a financial crisis (e.g., eviction from apartment, being threatened with repossession by creditors). While some emergencies are inevitable, these situations are generally the culmination of a long pattern of financial problems. The costs of these crises are large. First, they are stressful and disruptive for the members and their families. Second, the military incurs extra costs for shipping the members home, is shorthanded for the deployment, and reaps little return on predeployment training costs.

Since financial problems have implications for the workplace, the military services have traditionally played an active role in helping members with managing their finances. The services provide formal classes on personal financial management. Unit NCOs also provide advice and encourage members to keep their finances in order. Creditors frequently contact NCOs about debt problems, and the NCOs pressure members to meet their financial obligations.[2] Loans and financial counseling are available for members with problems.

GOALS OF THIS RESEARCH

This report examines the extent and composition of financial problems for junior enlisted members. We attempt to identify whether

---

[2]NCO involvement in financial issues is intended to ease member problems, but it may have the unintended effect of emboldening local merchants to make "risky" loans to servicemembers on the belief that the local NCO will ensure payment. Many NCOs resent the calls from local merchants and believe that it is the merchants' responsibility to collect from members. Nonetheless, most supervisors feel that they must act as a leader and pressure members to meet their financial obligations.

some types of members are more prone to financial distress than others. We also identify whether some military experiences (e.g., deployments or long hours) are associated with more problems than other experiences are. The analysis attempts to identify the reasons for underlying problems and target groups of members at greatest risk for financial problems.

STRUCTURE OF REPORT

The remainder of the report is divided into four chapters. Chapter Two provides an overview of data sources, service training programs, and financial measures used in the analysis. Chapter Three compares the extent of personal financial problems for similar military and civilian individuals. The analysis examines whether the incidence of serious financial problems is similar between military and civilian populations. The results also identify which types of individuals are having financial problems in both groups. Chapter Four focuses on how military-related factors affect financial problems of servicemembers. The analysis describes the relationships between various military situations (e.g., deployments or living in on-base housing) and an individual's financial condition. The final chapter summarizes the results and makes policy recommendations.

Chapter Two

DATA SOURCES, PROGRAMS, AND MEASURES
OF FINANCIAL PROBLEMS

This chapter reviews the sources of our data, describes financial management programs available to members, and examines various measures used to gauge the extent of the financial problems among junior enlisted personnel.

FOCUS GROUPS AND INTERVIEWS

To gain insight into the type of financial problems that junior enlisted personnel experience, we visited seven military bases and spoke with more than 300 people, including junior enlisted members, unit leaders, personnel support officials, financial management instructors, and base commanders. We made informal visits to Fort Drum, New York (Army); Camp Pendleton, California (Marine Corps); and Edwards AFB, California (Air Force) to discuss financial problems with personal support managers and base officials. We followed up these visits with four intensive three-day visits to Fort Lewis, Washington (Army); San Diego, California (Navy); Offutt AFB, Nebraska (Air Force); and Camp Lejeune, North Carolina (Marine Corps). In these longer visits, we conducted focus groups with junior enlisted personnel as well as with supervisors (platoon and company sergeants and commanders or the relevant comparable groups for the given service).

Military leaders held the common view that financial problems were the main problem facing junior enlisted personnel. Unit leaders consistently complained that much of their time was spent dealing directly with financially overextended members. These problems had a corrosive effect on the unit because they affected work performance through added stress on members as well as through absences to deal with creditors or get credit counseling.

The common explanation advanced for the prevalence of financial problems was that the junior enlisted personnel are financially naive. Many young enlisted members do not anticipate the consequences of acquiring debt or paying off debts at high interest rates. Purchase decisions are made piecemeal without concern for their cumulative effect on family budgets. Easy availability of credit and credit cards enables members to live beyond their means for a while, but the short-term extravagance then creates a crisis to pay off the bills.

The problem of financial naiveté can be exacerbated by the fact that many junior enlisted marry and start families at a young age. The members are not accustomed to budgeting their own funds and are sometimes unable to manage the extra complexity of a household budget. In addition, many young couples do not communicate well with one another about financial matters. Some partners spend independently without negotiating (or even discussing) a family budget or spending priorities. These spending patterns often culminate in the family being unable to meet financial obligations.

Young civilian adults have similar problems, but the military differs in at least two ways that have important ramifications for financial issues. First, young military members frequently are far away from their families. Older siblings and parents can help young adults monitor their finances through their advice and shared experiences. Military members miss this mentoring by living at a base distant from their relatives. Second, many local merchants take advantage of the limited financial skills of young members. These merchants offer cars, stereos, electronics, and furniture for little or no money down but charge high rates of interest. The members are sometimes naive about the actual cost of the purchase and its effect on their monthly budgets.

An overly simplistic explanation of members' higher tendency for having financial problems (Luther et al., 1997) is that low pay causes them. As we discuss below, the level of pay does not seem to correlate with financial problems. Furthermore, even if this correlation existed, this argument prompts the question of why people join or remain in the military if they had more lucrative options elsewhere. Their continued participation in the military suggests that many members see their military jobs and benefits as at least equal to those of civilian employment. Thus, military pay/compensation is already competitive. A recent analysis of military and civilian pay tends to confirm that judgment. It found that military personnel were in the seventieth to eightieth percentiles of pay for individuals with comparable education and experience (Asch and Hosek, 1999).

PROGRAMS

The military services have traditionally provided a variety of formal and informal programs to address members' financial problems. Unit leaders are a primary source of financial advice for junior enlisted members. The leaders recognize how financial matters affect performance and counsel members on avoiding problems. Local creditors sometimes contact leaders about delinquent bills and ask the leaders to help assure them that the member will meet his or her financial obligations. Many leaders are frustrated that their efforts in resolving delinquent bills encourage merchants to offer members credit on items that the members cannot afford.

The services also offer classes in personal financial management issues. These classes offer instruction on check balancing, budgeting, and credit issues. The classes also help members identify when they are having problems through a series of financial checkups. In addition to the classes, individualized financial counseling is available to members for special problems or circumstances.[1]

In recent years, the emphasis of formal financial training has increased. The Air Force required all personnel to receive financial management training at first assignment, starting in February 1997 (Stone, 1998), and other services have also revamped their classroom courses. Online assistance was initiated in September 1997 through

---

[1]Many personnel-support programs are underutilized because "needy" members are not knowledgeable about their availability (Buddin, 1998; Segal and Harris, 1993). Segal and Harris (1993) found that knowledge of financial management classes was widespread among members. Similarly, in our focus groups, members were aware of financial management training available at their bases.

the DoD Military Assistance Program Web site that provided online financial management advice to military members and their families. A recent congressional commission recommended a financial management class for all members during the first six months of service and a mandatory annual follow-up class for the first four years of military service (Report, 1999). DoD has accepted these recommendations and intensified classroom training in financial management issues.

Personnel support managers see the courses as a critical approach to aggressively solving members' financial problems. Members are reluctant to seek help for financial problems and generally only sought advice in a financial crisis (generally on orders from their unit). While one-on-one advice is useful in these emergencies, the solutions are more draconian than the options at earlier stages of a financial struggle. The classes show members principles of financial management and alert them to risky behaviors.

Members are frequently frustrated with financial management and other classes, because they do not seem useful and are another task added to a long work schedule. The common complaint is that all members are punished for the problems of few. In addition, the class material may have little salience for members who are not currently having problems. Members would prefer a more focused approach that provided help when needed. On the other hand, members are reluctant to seek financial advice, because a stigma is associated with needing financial help. This problem is compounded by the members' need for permission from unit leaders to get time off for financial counseling.[2]

SURVEY DATA ON FINANCIAL MANAGEMENT

We drew our data from three sources. For military personnel, the 1999 Active-Duty Survey (ADS) was the main source of data for our analysis (Wright et al., 2000). The survey was fielded late in 1999 and collected information on a random sample of enlisted and officer

---

[2]In many cases, the members may miss a scheduled day in the field, so they can meet a counseling appointment. This leaves the unit shorthanded and draws attention to the member's financial situation.

personnel in all service branches. We participated in the selection of questions for the survey and proposed a series of financial management questions, based on our previous survey and analysis of these problems (Tiemeyer et al., 1999). In addition to the financial questions, the survey contains information on a broad set of member demographics, service experiences, and individual attitudes. The survey had about 36,000 respondents, and our analysis is based on 8,000 respondents who are enlisted personnel with 10 or less years of military service.[3]

The second data source was the RAND 1997 Enlisted Career Intentions (ECI) Survey (Tiemeyer et al., 1999). This survey was restricted to enlisted members with 10 or less years of service. The data set contains a random sample of 6,200 observations. The ECI was a prototype survey that explored various dimensions of the reenlistment decision for junior enlisted personnel. A key feature of the survey was to design questions comparable to existing civilian surveys. We designed a small set of questions for the survey on the financial status of members. A portion of these questions was repeated in the 1999 ADS survey and allows us to compare the extent of financial problems between 1997 and 1999.

The ADS and ECI are random samples of military personnel, but they do not longitudinally track the same individuals. The ADS sampling strategy did not focus on individuals who participated in the ECI survey. It would be useful to know whether an individual who had financial problems in 1997 continued to have them in 1999. The files cannot be linked, however, so this type of tracking is not possible.

Civilian data for our analysis were drawn from the 1996 Panel Study of Income Dynamics (PSID). The PSID is a nationally representative sample of individuals. The survey is longitudinal and has been conducted annually since 1968. For our purposes, we wanted a sample of civilians roughly comparable to junior enlisted personnel, so we excluded civilians who were full-time students or over the age of 40. The PSID sample consists of 1,465 individuals.

---

[3]The ADS contains information that could be used to examine financial problems for enlisted personnel with more than 10 years of service and officers. The analysis of these groups was beyond the scope of this project.

Each survey is based on a complex design that oversamples some population groups and undersamples others. This stratified random sampling strategy is used to improve the precision of the estimates for some population groups. For example, the surveys oversample minority youth so the estimated characteristics of these groups can be more accurately measured than from a simpler design of random sampling. Because some types of individuals were oversampled, all observations were weighted according to their actual proportion in the overall military or civilian population. For example, women were oversampled in the military surveys to gain better measurements of their responses. However, this leads to their being overrepresented in the data set. To compensate, female respondents have a lower weight than do male respondents. This not only allows a more accurate assessment of the female recruit, but also provides an accurate overall representation of the entire enlisted military population.

A comparable set of variables was constructed for the three data sets, and these working data sets were merged into one master data set. The merged data allows us to compare the extent of military and civilian financial problems for adjacent years (1996 and 1997) as well as to assess any possible trends in military problems between 1997 and 1999. Ideally, we would have contemporaneous measures of military and civilian groups for multiple years. This type of detail is not available.

The military services intensified their personal financial management courses over this time period, so our analysis provides some insight into whether the new courses are reducing financial problems for military members. Of course, it is difficult to disentangle effects of the new programs from other trends in the economy and spending behavior of members. A better approach for measuring program effects would have been a phased implementation of the new programs, so the success (or failure) of the programs could be compared between experimental and control sites.

MEASURES OF FINANCIAL PROBLEMS

The military surveys contain information about individuals' subjective perceptions of their financial condition as well as an objective measure of their financial problems. The PSID only contains information about specific financial problems faced by the individual in the past year. None of these surveys, however, provide a systematic financial audit of the individuals or families.

Many junior enlisted members are concerned about their financial status. Figure 2.1 shows that 4 percent of members described themselves as "in over their head" and another 20 percent found it "tough to make ends meet."

A weakness with this measure of financial condition is that it is completely subjective. A financial audit of members may show that some are in financial distress but are not aware of the problem. Similarly, some of those with concerns could be overreacting to a minor or transitory situation. An audit might identify a different ranking of problems among members than does the self-report.

On the other hand, a self-reported financial condition may be a useful measure because it reflects the individual concerns and stresses

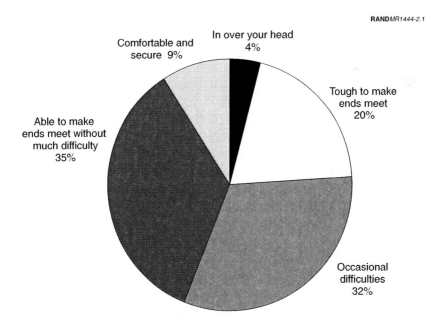

RAND*MR1444-2.1*

Figure 2.1—Self-Reported Financial Condition of Military Members in 1999

that face a member. This stress may affect work performance and family relationships. Thus, the subjective measure is an important indication of problems even if the underlying financial problems are not large by some objective standard.

The ECI and ADS surveys also contain information about specific financial problems that individuals faced in the past year. Figure 2.2 shows that many enlisted members had serious problems meeting their financial obligations. About 16 percent of members were pressured to pay bills by stores, creditors, or bill collectors. About 10 percent of members had utilities (telephone, cable, water, heat, or electricity) shut off during the past year. Another 9 percent pawned or sold off valuables to make ends meet. While many members live on base and pay no monthly rent, 7 percent of off-base members fell behind during the past year in paying the rent or mortgage. Only about 1 percent of members had items repossessed or filed for bankruptcy.

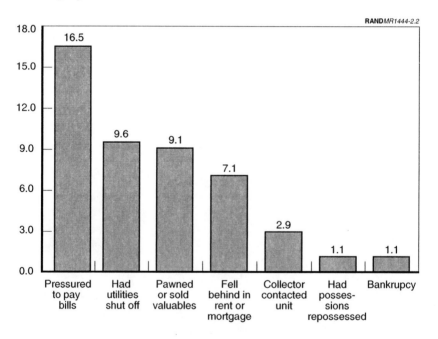

Figure 2.2—Financial Problems Among Enlisted Members During the Past 12 Months, 1999

The objective evidence on specific problems is consistent with the subjective reports of financial problems. About 26 percent of members had at least one of the serious problems in paying bills described in Figure 2.2. Figure 2.3 shows that the incidence of problems is much larger for members with concerns about their finances than for other members. More than three-fourths of those who reported being in over their heads faced a serious problem paying bills in the past year, compared with only 4 percent of those who felt comfortable and secure about their financial condition. On the other hand, one-fourth of those who were "in over their heads" did not report any serious bill problems. These individuals may still have serious financial difficulties, but they are scrupulously limiting their spending and paying bills on time.

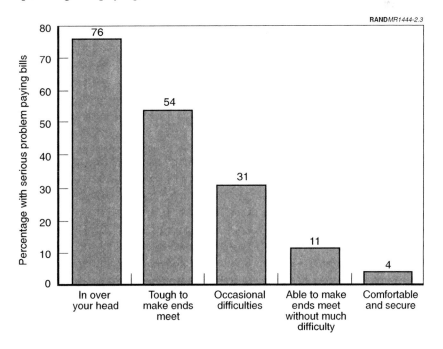

RAND*MR1444-2.3*

Financial Condition

Figure 2.3—Extent of Financial Problems by Member's Financial Condition, 1999

A comprehensive review of personal financial problems would include a complete audit of individual financial assets, savings, and debts. This objective information provides a more complete picture of the individual's financial condition. For example, debts or problems in paying short-term debts are probably less important for an individual with large assets or savings base than for an individual who has little or no equity. The Survey of Consumer Finance (SCF) collects this type of information for civilians (Kennickell et al., 2000). The key measures of financial problems for the SCF are the debt-to-income and debt-to-asset ratios. Unfortunately, no similar data are available for military personnel.

A financial audit was not included in the 1999 ADS because this detail would have "crowded out" other issues on this multipurpose survey. Also, legitimate concerns arose about whether the members would provide financial detail for privacy reasons. The ADS has little information on individual assets. It does include a couple of savings and debt questions, but the responses are defined as broad categories. The information on the survey was insufficient to make comparisons of the debt-to-income or debt-to-asset ratios for civilians in the SCF and military members in the ADS.

Chapter Three

COMPARISON OF MILITARY AND CIVILIAN FINANCIAL PROBLEMS

How do the financial problems of military members compare with those of their civilian counterparts? A comparison of financial problems between junior enlisted members and their civilian counterparts may provide some insight into the dimensions of military member's financial problems. The military is a somewhat unusual employer in that it hires primarily young, untrained, entry-level employees. If financial turmoil is widespread among the young, inexperienced workforce, then high levels of financial distress may be an inevitable consequence of the underlying military manning philosophy. Alternatively, unique military duties, responsibilities, and living situations may strain the financial management skills of members.

This chapter is divided into three parts. The first part describes simple differences between the civilian and military data sets. This description highlights demographic and other factors that may affect the financial situation of individuals and families. The second part examines whether military status has a significant effect on financial problems after controlling for a variety of demographic and family factors. The results show whether military members are more likely than civilians to have faced pressure from creditors to pay bills in the past, after adjusting for other factors that may be related to financial problems. The third part is similar to the second, but it focuses on a broader measure of financial problems—difficulty in paying bills when they are due. The analysis also shows how financial problems vary with demographics and family situation for the civilian and military populations.

DESCRIPTION OF MERGED DATA SET

Table 3.1 shows the means and proportions for each sample in the merged data set. The PSID data are drawn from the 1996 Family Survey. The PSID follows the traditional census-based approach of defining the husband as the head of household in intact husband-wife families. Under this approach, single and married men are defined as heads of household. Single women are heads of household, but a married woman is considered to be a member of her husband's household. The ECI and ADS samples are based on participation of an individual in the military (without regard to household status), but the surveys do include information on the characteristics of the military spouse. For conformity with the PSID coding, the ECI and ADS characteristics are defined as those of the head of household for married women. The means and proportions reflect the head-of-household characteristics except for the monthly family income variable, which includes the income for all members of the household.

As expected, small differences in the composition of military cropped up between 1997 and 1999. Most variables have similar means or proportions for the two years. The education composition did change somewhat between the two years: The proportion with at least some college (which includes associate's and bachelor's degree holders) rose from 0.54 in 1997 to 0.62 in 1999. The services have intensified their efforts to recruit college-bound youth and are encouraging members to attend college classes while in the military. This large difference, however, may also reflect more subtle changes in the way the surveys were administered. The ECI shows a slightly larger proportion of members with children than the ADS (0.36 as compared with 0.32), but the number of children varies substantially between the two surveys. The ECI reports 21 percent of members with one child compared with only 11 percent in the ADS.

The differences between the military and civilian samples are more substantial. The civilian sample is much older and better-educated than the military samples. The military recruits young, entry-level employees for the enlisted force, so these differences are not surprising. The other large difference between the groups is the higher and more widely dispersed monthly family income for civilian house-

Table 3.1

Means and Proportions for Variables in Merged
PSID, ECI, and ADS Data Set

Characteristic	Civilian	Military	
	PSID (1996)	ECI (1997)	ADS (1999)
Age	31.42	24.00	24.08
Female	0.23	0.08	0.09
Male	0.77	0.92	0.91
Black	0.11	0.18	0.15
Hispanic	0.05	0.10	0.14
White Non-Hispanic	0.84	0.72	0.71
No college	0.45	0.46	0.38
Some college	0.24	0.37	0.51
Associate's degree	0.04	0.12	0.07
Bachelor's degree	0.27	0.05	0.04
Single	0.35	0.40	0.46
Divorced	0.12	0.05	0.05
Married	0.53	0.55	0.49
One child	0.17	0.21	0.11
Two children	0.21	0.11	0.08
Three or more children	0.11	0.04	0.13
Child less than age five	0.26	0.29	0.28
Family income per month			
$1–1,000	0.03	NA	0.06
$1,001–2,000	0.16	NA	0.56
$2,001–3,000	0.20	NA	0.25
$3,001–4,000	0.21	NA	0.08
$4,001–5,000	0.13	NA	0.03
$5,001 and above	0.26	NA	0.02
Military affiliation			
Army	NA	0.35	0.37
Navy	NA	0.29	0.26
Air Force	NA	0.21	0.22
Marine Corps	NA	0.15	0.15
Measures of financial problems			
Pressured by creditors	0.08	0.22	0.18
Serious difficulty paying bills	0.16	0.29	0.29
Sample size	1,465	6,263	7,904

NOTE: The ECI did not ask about family income.

holds than for military households.[1] Two factors suggest that these differences are closely related to the differences in age and education between the two groups. First, income rises sharply with experience during early years in the workforce, so the younger military members earn more as they gain more labor market experience. Second, there is a substantial wage premium for a bachelor's degree. This premium contributes to the higher level of earnings for civilians, because many in the civilian data set have a bachelor's degree. Also, greater variance in educational attainment for civilians than for the enlisted members contributes to the greater variance in family income.

An important weakness of the ADS is that the categorical income groups are not well chosen. Thousand-dollar-per-month income brackets are quite large, and 81 percent of junior enlisted members fall into two brackets (57 percent of members have monthly family income between $1,001 and $2,000). These broad brackets collapse the variance in income and make it difficult to detect whether income affects financial problems or other issues. In future surveys, the quality of the income variable (and subsequent data analysis) would be considerably enhanced by a continuous measure of family income or an improved categorical variable with smaller intervals in the range of most respondent's income.

Financial problems vary substantially between the military and civilian groups but much less between military members in 1997 and 1999. Only about 8 percent of civilians were pressured by creditors to pay bills during the past year, compared with 22 percent of military members in 1997 and 18 percent of military members in 1999. About 16 percent of civilians had serious problems paying bills during the past year, compared with 29 percent of military members in both 1997 and 1999.

The simple tabulations of financial problems may be a misleading indication of financial problems for military members, because they neglect the differences in the compositions of the military and civilian workforces. Better-educated and older civilians may have fewer

---

[1]The ECI did not collect information on family income. The PSID has a continuous measure of family income. For the comparison with the ADS, family income was converted into 1999 dollars and coded into the categories available on the ADS.

problems than military members because of their training and maturity. The observed differences in financial problems between military and civilian populations may reflect differences in the composition of the two groups and not differences in underlying behavior. The next two parts of this section examine the incidence of financial problems for the military and civilian sectors, adjusting for the demographic and other factors in Table 3.1 that may also affect family finances.

PRESSURED BY CREDITORS

Table 3.2 describes how military status, demographics, and family situations affect the probability that an individual or family was pressured by creditors to pay bills in the past year. The results of three sets of regression models are shown: civilian versus military (all services combined), civilian versus military service branch, civilian versus military service branch with family income as an additional control. For all of the regression models, the civilian group was used as the base for comparison. Two types of entries are reported in Table 3.2 for the effect of a change in a characteristic on the underlying probability of the incidence of a financial problem (dF/dX). For continuous variables, such as age, the table shows the change in the probability of having problems with respect to the attribute. Thus, the age effect means that a one-year increment in an individual's age is associated with a 0.58 percentage point decline in the probability of facing pressure from creditors. The predicted change is predicated on comparing individuals who are average in all other respects and differ only in age. Many of the variables are discrete indicator variables (e.g., female or male head of household), and, in this case, the entries show the percentage point change between the particular category and the underlying reference category. For example, the results suggest that the predicted probability of a female head of household having problems with creditors is 6.09 percentage points higher than for an otherwise similar male head-of-household.

The reference group for the regression is married, male, white non-Hispanic high school graduates with no children (and family income of $1,001 to $2,000 per month in the third regression). Entries are not reported for these groups in Table 3.2, because the reported entries

Table 3.2

Effects of Demographic and Family Factors on Probability of Being
Pressured by Creditors to Pay Bills

Characteristic	Civilian Versus Military		Civilian Versus Each Service		Civilian Versus Military with Family Income	
	dF/dX	Standard Error	dF/dX	Standard Error	dF/dX	Standard Error
Age	−0.0058*	0.0011	−0.0061*	0.0011	−0.0033*	0.0012
Female	0.0609	0.0494	0.0613	0.0492	0.0416	0.0441
Female and military	−0.0450	0.0379	−0.0403	0.0382	−0.0398	0.0354
Hispanic	0.0038	0.0127	−0.0022	0.0124	−0.0006	0.0138
Black	0.0618*	0.0114	0.0534*	0.0113	0.0641*	0.0144
Some college	−0.0361*	0.0083	−0.0301*	0.0084	−0.0254*	0.0099
Associate's degree	−0.0836*	0.0110	−0.0775*	0.0113	−0.0861*	0.0123
Bachelor's degree	−0.1012*	0.0134	−0.1001*	0.0133	−0.0965*	0.0137
Single	0.0556	0.0416	0.0543	0.0412	0.0310	0.0381
Single and military	−0.0890*	0.0381	−0.0882*	0.0377	−0.0859*	0.0348
Divorced	0.0519*	0.0193	0.0548*	0.0194	0.0253	0.0214
One child	−0.0029	0.0183	−0.0033	0.0182	0.0004	0.0229
Two children	0.0293	0.0216	0.0248	0.0214	0.0124	0.0255
Three or more children	0.0744*	0.0249	0.0681*	0.0247	0.0703*	0.0296
Child less than age five	0.0153	0.0176	0.0171	0.0176	0.0035	0.0212
Military in 1997	0.1863*	0.0249				
Military in 1999	0.1371*	0.0223			0.0928*	0.0161
Army in 1997			0.2325*	0.0339		
Navy in 1997			0.2041*	0.0333		
Air Force in 1997			0.1490*	0.0319		
Marine Corps in 1997			0.2358*	0.0375		
Army in 1999			0.2005*	0.0304		
Navy in 1999			0.1400*	0.0311		
Air Force in 1999			0.0673*	0.0298		
Marine Corps in 1999			0.1650*	0.0349		

Table 3.2—continued

Characteristic	Civilian Versus Military		Civilian Versus Each Service		Civilian Versus Military with Family Income	
	dF/dX	Standard Error	dF/dX	Standard Error	dF/dX	Standard Error
Family income per month						
$1–1,000					–0.0278	0.0221
$2,001–3,000					–0.0112	0.0117
$3,001–4,000					–0.0489*	0.0138
$4,001–5,000					–0.0698*	0.0165
$5,001 and above					–0.0654*	0.0201

NOTE: The first two regressions are based on a merged data set constructed from the PSID, ECI, and ADS data. The third regression omits ECI data because there is no family income measure in the ECI. The reference group for the regression is married, male, non-Hispanic high school graduates with no children (and family income of $1,001 to $2,000 per month in the third regression).

The estimated effects (dF/dX) correspond to changes in the probability relative to the excluded reference category for discrete variables and the derivative of the probability for continuous variables. Entries with asterisks are associated with effects that are significant at the $\alpha = 0.05$ confidence level.

are relative to these groups. For example, the second column shows that the probability of being pressured by creditors to pay bills is 0.38 and 6.18 percentage points higher in families with a Hispanic or black head of household than in an otherwise comparable family with a white non-Hispanic head of household.

The large and significant effects for military membership in Table 3.2 indicate that military members are much more prone to financial problems than otherwise comparable civilians are. The magnitude of these differences is shown in Figure 3.1. Consider a representative individual with the attributes of a military member in 1999. The figure shows how likely this individual is to have problems with creditors if the individual is civilian, a military member in 1997, or a military member in 1999. This exercise isolates the differences between military and civilian creditor problems, as well as the trend in military problems between 1997 and 1999.

Figure 3.1 shows that the percentage of creditor problems for military members is much higher than for comparable civilians. Even if

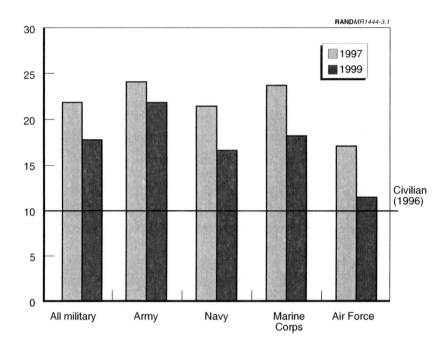

Figure 3.1—Military and Civilian Differences in Percentage of Individuals
Pressured by Creditors to Pay Bills (Adjusted for Demographic and
Family Factors)

Athe civilian workforce were similar to the military (e.g., younger and
with fewer college graduates), the results show that the civilian rate
of creditor problems would still be an order of magnitude less than
the military rate. Only 10 percent of comparable civilians have
problems compared with 23 and 18 percent of military members in
1997 and 1999, respectively.

mong the service branches, the Army and Marine Corps members
have greater difficulties than Navy and Air Force, even after adjusting
for differences in the demographics and family characteristics of
members in each service. The Air Force rates are closest to those of
the civilian workforce, and the 1999 Air Force rate is only 1.5 percentage points higher than the comparable civilian rate. We will look
at these service differences in financial problems again in the next
chapter to see whether the patterns correspond to a military envi-

ronment (e.g., deployments, assignment patterns, or work schedule) that may create extra problems for Army and Marine Corps personnel.

Figure 3.1 does show a substantial decline in members facing pressure from creditors between 1997 and 1999. The overall military rate fell by 5 percentage points in two years, and each service had a large decline in members with this financial problem. These gains might indicate that increased service emphasis on financial management problems is paying some dividends. The other possibility is that the improvement may be related to a stronger civilian economy or some unrelated trend in financial behavior. A strong economy might help military spouses find better jobs or members find better part-time employment in the civilian sector. Lower interest rates in 1999 might also ease member expenses in paying of debts. A useful baseline comparison would be the changes in civilians with pressure from creditors between 1996 and 1999. Unfortunately, no civilian data have comparable information for 1999, so it is unclear what the military reductions in problems between 1997 and 1999 mean.

The effect of demographics and family factors is consistent across military and civilian groups as well as across military members in the two years. The effects of age or ethnicity or the presence of children on family financial problems is consistent across the PSID, ECI, and ADS. The results suggest that the effects of all variables vary insignificantly between military members in the two years. Two civilian/military interactions are important: female heads of household in the military are less prone to have financial problems than their civilian counterparts, and single individuals in the military are less prone to problems than otherwise comparable civilians.[2] These interactions are discussed in more detail below.

The probability of creditor problems declines with age and education. More-experienced and higher-skilled individuals may be more likely to avoid spending sprees or better able to budget for unexpected expenses. The age effect is quite modest because each year of

_____

[2]The "female and military" interaction is statistically insignificant in Table 3.1, but the interaction is significant in explaining whether individuals have serious difficulties paying bills (see Chapter Four). The insignificant interaction is reported here for consistency with the specification later in the paper.

age only reduces the probability of problems by 0.58 percentage points.[3] Individuals with some college, an associate's degree, or a college degree are 4, 8, and 10 percentage points less likely to have financial difficulties than similar individuals with no college attendance.

A female-headed civilian household is 6 percentage points more likely to have pressure from creditors than is a similar male-headed civilian household. An interesting result is that, among military members, females are no more likely than males to have financial problems from creditors. While the civilian gender gap in financial difficulties does not exist in the military, military women still have a much higher rate of pressure from creditors than their civilian counterparts.

Among civilians and military members, blacks have higher rates of financial problems than both Hispanics and white non-Hispanics. Military members who are black, Hispanic, and white non-Hispanic have higher rates of financial problem than their civilian counterparts, but the military effect does not vary with the race/ethnicity effect.

Marriage and divorce are both likely to increase financial problems. Financial coordination is easier for a single individual than for a couple. Most young adults find that spending pressures increase with marriage. Divorced individuals incur extra expenses for maintaining or establishing two households. Also, financial problems are a frequent precursor of marital breakups, so divorcees may have residual financial burdens to deal with.

Figure 3.2 shows that the relationship between marital status and financial problems differs between the civilian and military sectors.[4]

----

[3]In earlier specifications, we included a quadratic age variable along with the linear variable. Our hypothesis is that financial problems would decline with age at a decreasing rate. The coefficient on the quadratic variable was not statistically significant, however, so we reported the results from the simpler specification with a linear age variable.

[4]The civilian and military comparisons are based on the assumption that an individual with the average characteristics of a military member in 1999 was in each marital status group. The comparison is intended to isolate marital status effects, so the number of children is set at zero.

Among civilians, married adults have fewer problems than single or divorced adults do. At each marital status, military members have a higher rate of problems than do comparable civilians, but the pattern of problems across marital status differs for the two groups. About 14 percent of single military members have been pressured by creditors to pay bills, compared with 18 percent of married members and 23 percent of divorced members. The incidence of creditor problems is lower for married civilians (8 percent) than for either single or divorced civilians (11 percent).

The relatively low rates of problems for single members may reflect the fact that most of them live in on-base barracks housing and eat in a military dining facility. These food and shelter benefits are provided in-kind, so single members do not have to budget for these

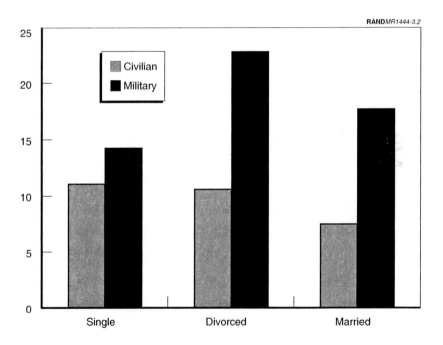

RAND*MR1444-3.2*

Figure 3.2—Marital Status Differences in Percentage of Individuals Pressured by Creditors to Pay Bills by Civilian and Military Individuals (Adjusted for Demographic and Family Factors)

basics. Some married members live in on-base housing at no cost. Most live off base, however, and receive a housing allowance to defray costs. Married members receive a monetary subsistence allowance each month to cover food expenses. Budgeting is more complex for members with families because they have more decisions to make about housing and food expenses. This complexity may explain why married members have greater financial problems than do single members.

Divorced military members are having many financial problems and are facing substantial pressure from creditors. The extra costs of maintaining or at least contributing to two households may be a burden, but the relative burden is much greater for military than for civilian individuals. This gap may reflect the fact that military assignment patterns mean that military members are much more likely than civilians to live away from their children and incur extra costs for visits or long-distance phone calls.

Children may strain family resources by increasing the need for a larger dwelling and by incurring extra child expenses. Children may also increase the complexity of family budgeting, because childhood illnesses may create unexpected medical expenses or unpaid employment absences.

The results in Table 3.2 indicate that financial problems do not increase significantly for families with one or two children, but they do increase for larger families. Families with three or more children are 7 percentage points more likely to be pressured by creditors than are comparable families with no children.

Young children may put financial pressure on families for child-care expenses or by reducing earnings of a parent caregiver. The results show that families with young children do not have greater financial problems than other families, however. Apparently, military and civilian parents with young children are able (on average) to balance the various demands on their household finances and avoid serious creditor problems.

The final specification in Table 3.2 adds family income to the demographic and family variables in the model. This specification is intended to identify whether family income is an important factor in financial difficulties. Are financial problems concentrated in low-income groups or are they more pervasive? The problem with including family income in the specification is that income is endogenous and reflects a series of decisions by the family. For example, a family may seek out extra income through a second job or spouse employment, because they face severe financial difficulties. This extra complexity means that the income effect in the table may reflect a variety of factors related to household decisions to work and not the effect of income per se.

The results show that financial problems are not strongly related to family income, especially over the range of most military incomes. The probability that an individual or family faced pressure from creditors to pay bills does not vary significantly over the range of monthly incomes of less than $3,000, which accounts for about 87 percent of the range of military members' incomes. Financial problems are 4 to 7 percentage points lower for families with incomes greater than $3,000 than for those with incomes less than $3,000 per month.

The pattern of significant coefficients in Table 3.2 remains similar after controlling for family income, but the magnitude of the effects is somewhat weakened. Military members are still twice as likely as civilians to have financial problems.

SERIOUS DIFFICULTY IN PAYING BILLS

Many individuals face serious problems paying bills in addition to being pressured by creditors. These problems include involuntarily having the utilities shut off, pawning and selling valuables to pay bills, falling behind in rent or mortgage, having goods repossessed, and filing for bankruptcy. These types of problems reflect a serious difficulty in paying bills when they are due.

Table 3.3 shows how difficulty in paying bills varies with military status, demographics, and family characteristics. Difficulties with paying bills in the past year are more widespread than the narrower category of being pressured by creditors to pay bills described in the last section. Some individuals or families who do not report specific pressure from creditors to pay bills do fall behind in the rent or have utilities shut off.

Table 3.3

Effects of Demographic and Family Factors on Probability of Serious Difficulty in Paying Bills

Characteristic	Civilian Versus Military		Civilian Versus Each Service		Civilian Versus Military with Family Income	
	dF/dX	Standard Error	dF/dX	Standard Error	dF/dX	Standard Error
Age	−0.0081*	0.0013	−0.0085*	0.0013	−0.0058*	0.0015
Female	0.1155*	0.0492	0.1154*	0.0491	0.0815	0.0489
Female and military	−0.1005*	0.0358	−0.0938*	0.0363	−0.0906*	0.0371
Hispanic	−0.0013	0.0143	−0.0106	0.0141	−0.0034	0.0169
Black	0.0579*	0.0125	0.0461*	0.0125	0.0690*	0.0163
Some college	−0.0463*	0.0096	−0.0386*	0.0097	−0.0344*	0.0121
Associate's degree	−0.0931*	0.0140	−0.0847*	0.0144	−0.1038*	0.0180
Bachelor's degree	−0.1297*	0.0167	−0.1290*	0.0167	−0.1386*	0.0183
Single	0.0880*	0.0412	0.0867*	0.0410	0.0483	0.0412
Single and military	−0.1330*	0.0382	−0.1318*	0.0380	−0.1118*	0.0388
Divorced	0.0918*	0.0219	0.0954*	0.0219	0.0539*	0.0263
One child	0.0378	0.0218	0.0377	0.0219	0.0462	0.0289
Two children	0.0840*	0.0247	0.0777*	0.0247	0.0764*	0.0315
Three or more children	0.1222*	0.0271	0.1153*	0.0272	0.1303*	0.0338
Child less than age five	0.0006	0.0192	0.0034	0.0193	−0.0138	0.0243
Military in 1997	0.1767*	0.0246				
Military in 1999	0.1656*	0.0228			0.0942*	0.0214
Army in 1997			0.2229*	0.0309		
Navy in 1997			0.1776*	0.0303		
Air Force in 1997			0.1139*	0.0290		
Marine Corps in 1997			0.1941*	0.0338		
Army in 1999			0.2394*	0.0281		
Navy in 1999			0.1419*	0.0292		
Air Force in 1999			0.0724*	0.0295		
Marine Corps in 1999			0.2039*	0.0328		

Table 3.3—continued

Characteristic	Civilian Versus Military		Civilian Versus Each Service		Civilian Versus Military with Family Income	
	dF/dX	Standard Error	dF/dX	Standard Error	dF/dX	Standard Error
Family income per month						
$1–1,000					−0.0290	0.0274
$2,001–3,000					−0.0247	0.0140
$3,001–4,000					−0.0890*	0.0168
$4,001–5,000					−0.1237*	0.0197
$5,001 and above					−0.1552*	0.0212

NOTE: The first two regressions are based on a merged data set constructed from the PSID, ECI, and ADS data. The third regression omits ECI data because there is no family income measure in the ECI. The reference group for the regression is married, male, non-Hispanic high school graduates with no children (and family income of $1,001 to $2,000 per month in the third regression).

The estimated effects (dF/dX) correspond to changes in the probability relative to the excluded reference category for discrete variables and the derivative of the probability for continuous variables. Entries with asterisks are associated with effects that are significant at the $\alpha = 0.05$ confidence level.

Figure 3.3 shows that the incidence of bill problems is much higher for military members than for comparable civilians. The "all military" column indicates that about 27 percent of military members have serious problems paying bills compared with 18.6 percent of civilians.[5] Financial difficulties are greater in the Army and Marine Corps than in the Navy and Air Force (even after adjusting for demographic differences of the individuals serving in these military branches). In the Air Force, the rate of bill problems in 1999 is similar to that of comparable civilians (as measured in 1996).

The overall military rate did not vary significantly between 1997 and 1999. The Navy and Air Force had statistically significant reductions in bill problems between 1997 and 1999. The incidence of problems rose slightly over this period in the Army and Marine Corps, but these changes are not statistically significant.

---

[5]The rate of bill problems here (18.6) is higher than the overall civilian rate of 16.0 in Table 3.1 because prediction is made for a set of civilians with demographics and family characteristics similar to the military population.

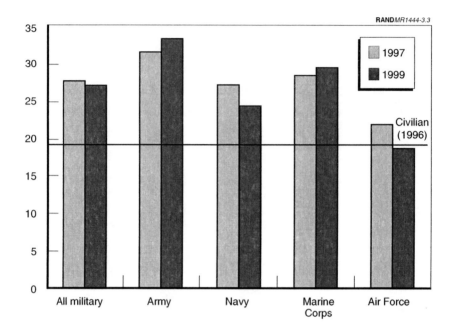

Figure 3.3—Military and Civilian Differences in Percentage of Individuals
with Serious Difficulty in Paying Bills (Adjusted
for Demographic and Family Factors)

A subtle alteration in the survey question has important implications for the rate of bill-paying problems reported in Figure 3.3. In 1999, the question about utility shutoffs mentions in parentheses "telephone, cable, water, heat, or electricity" as compared with the earlier question which asked about "water, heat, or electricity." Respondents could have included telephone or cable television problems in either case, but the 1999 wording prompts them for these issues.

The incidence of utility shutoffs for military members rose from 1 percent in 1997 to 10 percent in 1999. This tenfold increase probably reflects a substantial increase in coverage by adding the specific reference to telephone and cable problems.

The wording ambiguity in the two military questionnaires raises the rate of bill problems in the ADS compared with the ECI. The 1999 measure of bill problems probably includes some telephone and cable problems that had not been reported in the 1997 survey. Absent the extra telephone and cable problems, the military trend on serious problems in paying bills would show an improvement similar to the aforementioned trend in members facing pressure from creditors (Figure 3.1). The prevalence of bill problems in the military remains high, however, irrespective of which definition of utilities is used.

Demographic and family variables have a similar effect on bill problems to the narrower problem of pressure from creditors. Experience reduces problems by 0.8 percentage points per year of age. Financial problems are 5, 9, and 13 percentage points less common for individuals with some college, an associate's degree, or a bachelor's degree, respectively, than for individuals with no college training. Blacks are 6 percentage points more likely to have serious bill problems than comparable Hispanics or white non-Hispanics.

Figure 3.4 shows that the pattern of bill problems by gender differs between military and civilian households. Among civilians, about 22 percent of female-headed households have serious bill problems compared with only 13 percent of male-headed households. Military rates are higher than civilian for both female- and male-headed households at about 27 percent, but there is no gender gap for military households.

Figure 3.5 shows how marital status affects serious bill problems for both civilian and military households. About 20 percent of single and divorced civilians have problems paying bills compared with 13 percent of married civilians. In the military, about 22 percent of singles have bill problems as compared with 27 percent of married members and 36 percent of divorced members.

Serious bill problems do increase with family size for both civilian and military families. The incidence of bill-paying problems rises by about 4 percentage points per child. Having young children per se does not have any effect on the rate of bill problems for either civilian or military household, after adjusting for other factors and family size.

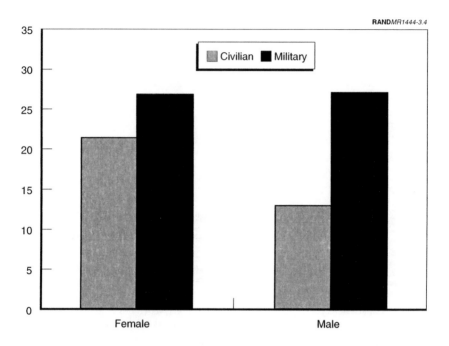

Figure 3.4—Percentage of Individuals with Serious Problems Paying Bills by Gender of Household Head and Military Status (Adjusted for Demographic and Family Factors)

The third regression model in Table 3.3 includes categories of family income. Financial problems do not vary with income over income classes associated with earnings of less than $3,000, which encompasses 87 percent of military families. For families with incomes greater than $3,000 a month, the incidence of serious bill problems is 8 to 15 percentage points lower than it is for families who earn $3,000 per month or less.

The inclusion of family income in the model reduces the magnitude of many other factors, but the pattern of significance changes little. Controlling for family income, financial difficulties are 10 percentage points higher for military families than for comparable civilian families.

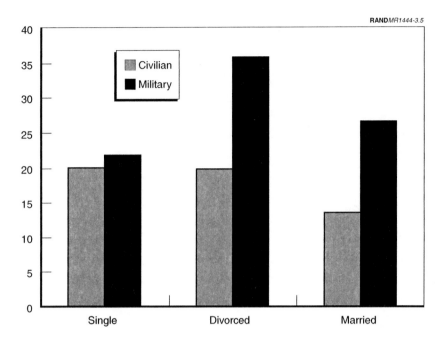

Figure 3.5—Percentage of Individuals with Serious Problems Paying Bills
by Marital Status of Household Head and Military Status (Adjusted for
Demographic and Family Factors)

Chapter Four

MILITARY ENVIRONMENT AND FINANCIAL PROBLEMS

This chapter delves into the financial problems of junior enlisted members further by examining possible contributing factors to financial instability unique to the military. Research questions include the following:

- How prevalent are financial problems among military members?

- Can they be considered serious problems?

- Do those in financially dire situations recognize their condition?

- Are there aspects unique to the military that contribute or alleviate tendencies for financial problems?

- Are there certain groups among the military more vulnerable to financial problems than others?

The analysis in this chapter relies on the 1999 ADS. As mentioned in Chapter Two, the ADS was conducted late in 1999 on a sample of officer and enlisted personnel in the Army, Air Force, Navy, and Marines. This analysis relies on a subset of the data corresponding to enlisted members with 10 or less years of military service.

MILITARY CHARACTERISTICS

To gain a better appreciation of the financial problems faced by members, a brief description/introduction to the unique aspects of the military is appropriate.

Because the military population is strikingly different from the civilian population, a brief sketch of the overall composition of military members may be helpful. Table 4.1 lists the weighted means and proportions for each characteristic, broken down by service, in the data set. Note that in addition to the typical variables that would be applicable to both the civilian and military population, attributes unique to the military are also included: deployment, on-base housing, country of post, etc.

As expected, military members are primarily young (19 to 29 years old) and overwhelmingly male. They are paid wages comparable to what they would receive for civilian employment, given their education and work experience (Asch and Hosek, 1999).

In addition to military pay, the military compensation system provides housing and subsistence benefits for military members that are rarely provided by civilian employers (Buddin et al., 1999). About half of members live in on-base housing. Most single members without children live in a dormitory-style barracks and eat at a military mess hall. These housing and subsistence benefits are provided in-kind at no cost to enlisted members. On-base family housing is offered at no cost (rent or utilities) to married and single parent members, subject to availability. These members receive a monthly subsistence allowance to defray food expenses. Members who live off base receive a monthly housing allowance to defray the cost of renting in the local community. The allowance is based on local rental prices and incorporates cost-of-living differences across bases. These members also receive a monthly subsistence allowances.

The housing and subsistence benefits mean that military members have extra funds over-and-above their military pay to cover these basic living expenses. These funds are explicitly paid to the off-base members and implicitly paid to on-base members through zero-price rent, utilities, and subsistence expenses. The value of the housing and subsistence benefits exceeds their nominal value because these benefits are not taxed.

These housing and subsistence benefits enhance member well-being and "free up" earnings for other expenditures. On-base members also benefit from not having to budget for housing and utility

Table 4.1

Weighted Means and Proportions for Variables in ADS Data Set

Characteristic	Army	Navy	Air Force	Marines
Age	24.81	24.01	24.03	22.38
Hispanic	0.14	0.13	0.09	0.18
Black	0.20	0.14	0.10	0.10
Female[a]	0.17	0.16	0.24	0.07
Some college	0.52	0.52	0.62	0.44
Associate's degree	0.08	0.05	0.11	0.04
Bachelor's degree	0.06	0.03	0.04	0.01
Single	0.42	0.52	0.47	0.56
Divorced	0.05	0.03	0.07	0.02
One child	0.12	0.10	0.16	0.09
Two children	0.10	0.07	0.08	0.06
Three or more children	0.17	0.14	0.10	0.09
Child less than age five	0.35	0.28	0.31	0.23
Family income per month				
$1–1,000	0.04	0.05	0.03	0.08
$1,001–2,000	0.54	0.51	0.54	0.61
$2,001–3,000	0.26	0.28	0.25	0.20
$3,001–4,000	0.09	0.09	0.09	0.06
$4,001–5,000	0.04	0.03	0.04	0.02
$5,001 and above	0.01	0.03	0.03	0.01
Deployed more than 30 days	0.65	0.45	0.39	0.57
Live on-base	0.67	0.50	0.60	0.73
Serve on ship	0.00	0.47	0.00	0.03
Spouse in military	0.06	0.02	0.11	0.03
Assigned to base in United States	0.77	0.86	0.81	0.87
Spouse has full-time civilian job[b]	0.16	0.17	0.15	0.14
Regularly exceed 50-hour workweek	0.64	0.53	0.27	0.61
Holds civilian job	0.11	0.14	0.16	0.11
Less than four years in military	0.64	0.64	0.59	0.79
Separated from spouse and child(ren)	0.05	0.02	0.02	0.04
Separated from spouse only	0.03	0.03	0.03	0.04
Separated from child(ren) only	0.03	0.03	0.02	0.03
Sample Size[c]	2,777	1,659	1,502	1,253

[a]The proportion indicates ratios of female members. This proportion differs from the female proportion in the ADS reported in Table 3.1 because the earlier table is based on head-of-household characteristics. Married female members are not heads of household; they are considered to be a part of their husband's household (to conform to the census-type definitions used by the PSID).

[b]This percentage is based on all members not just married members.

[c]Observations with missing information on military characteristics were dropped from the analysis in this chapter. As a result, the observation count is 713 observations smaller than those reported in Table 3.1. Sensitivity tests indicate that this did not discernibly change the results.

expenses. On-base members presumably face less pressure than civilians or off-base members to make their budgets balance because a major share of expenses (shelter and food) is automatically provided by the military. Even though on-base members are not concerned with basic food and shelter expenses, they still need to budget for miscellaneous expenses (e.g., telephone, entertainment, transportation, and clothes) judiciously.

As indicated in Table 4.1, mobility is a salient aspect of the military. Deployment for training and military missions is a normal obligation of military service. These deployments may be short term (less than a month) or long term (three to five months). Although the typical single deployment rarely exceeds six months, the total time deployed in a year may be much longer. The service with the fewest deployments, the Air Force, still reports 39 percent of their members being deployed for longer than one month in a 12-month period. The Army reports a substantial 65 percent of their members being deployed for longer than one month.

Reassignment to a different military base is also common, occurring about every three years. Members are assigned to particular posts for a specified period. At the end of that period, they receive new assignments that typically require moving. The military pays for many of the moving expenses, but many personnel managers believe that these moves put extra burdens on family finances (Tiemeyer et al., 1999). Families may need to make deposits for rent or utilities, replace belongings lost or damaged in the move, or incur other costs. Such expenses may stretch an already tight budget.

The remainder of this chapter explores how these types of military characteristics affect the financial situations of members. The analysis takes into consideration not only the demographics peculiar to the military population but also the unique or unusual aspects of duties involved in military service.

FINANCIAL SELF-ASSESSMENT

As discussed in Chapter Two, the ADS has two types of measures of a member's financial status: a subjective self-evaluation of the member's financial condition and a series of questions about specific difficulties in paying bills. Figure 4.1 shows that these two measures are pretty consistent for most members—i.e., most members who report having serious problems in paying bills over the past 12 months are concerned about their financial condition. Among those who have bill problems (e.g., falling behind in rent payments or experiencing general bill pressures) only 1 percent of them feel comfortable and secure in their financial position. More than 85 percent recognize that they have *at least* occasional difficulties in paying bills, and 11 percent believe that they are in deep financial trouble (in over your head).

In contrast, 12 percent of those who did not have bill-paying problems felt comfortable and secure and more than 50 percent of them believed they could at least make ends meet. Only 1 percent of these

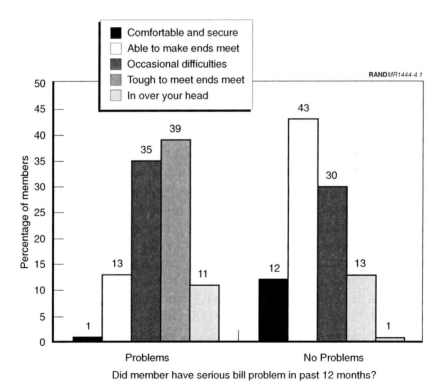

Figure 4.1—Financial Self-Assessment of Members With And Without Bill-Paying Problems

members considered themselves in over their heads. The distinct difference in distributions between those who had and those who did not have financial problems indicate that most members have financial self-perceptions that accurately stem from their actual financial condition; only a relatively small percentage of members have financial self-perceptions that do not seem to be supported by objective measurements.

Focusing on the members with fewer years in the military, we hypothesize that members who are younger, less experienced, and less accustomed to military work and life may be more vulnerable to organizational problems in budgeting their finances.

As Figure 4.2 indicates, a cursory examination between relatively new members serving four or less years and more experienced members who have served more than four years seems to imply little difference in their self-described financial conditions.

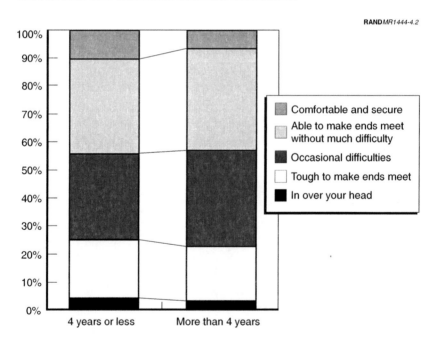

Figure 4.2—Breakdown of Financial Self-Assessment by Military Experience

An unexpected result is that a greater number of junior members regard themselves as financially secure than do more-experienced ones. Possible explanations include skewed expectations (younger, less-experienced members have not been out in the workforce long and simply have lower standards for feeling comfortable and secure), fewer dependents (younger, less-experienced members are less likely to be married and have fewer financial responsibilities), and unrealistic self-assessment (younger, less-experienced members are less likely to worry about the future and upcoming bills).

To help weed out these possible biases, the next section examines the incidence of financial problems, adjusting for demographic and military factors.

SERIOUS PROBLEMS IN PAYING BILLS

Serious problems in paying bills is defined as occurrences of falling behind in paying rent or mortgage; being pressured by bill collectors; pawning or selling valuables to make ends meet; having utilities shut off; having a car, household appliance, or furniture repossessed; being unable to afford needed medical care; and having a bill collector contacting unit leader.

Table 4.2 shows how various military factors, along with demographics and family characteristics, affect the probability of a member having serious problems in paying bills in the past year.

Three regression models were explored. The first set of columns show the results from the first regression model, which includes only demographic and family factors and excludes any controlling characteristic particular to the military. The second model includes military factors that may be negatively or positively associated with a member having financial problems. The coefficients included in the first model do not change remarkably in the second regression results. Most of the military coefficients are found to be statistically significant. The third model omits variables with possible endogeneity issues. For example, a member having a second, paying civilian job may introduce questions of reverse causality. A member with a second job may have unique characteristics (e.g., spending, work, or budgeting habits) that affect his or her financial status. On the other

Table 4.2

Effects of Military, Demographic, and Family Factors on Probability of Serious Difficulty in Paying Bills

Characteristic	Without Military Characteristics		With Military Characteristics		Excluding Suspect Variables	
	dF/dX	Standard Error	dF/dX	Standard Error	dF/dX	Standard Error
Age	−0.0057*	0.0016	−0.0034	0.0018	−0.0036*	0.0018
Hispanic	−0.0150	0.0154	−0.0110	0.0156	−0.0127	0.0154
Black	0.0463*	0.0158	0.0534*	0.0162	0.0459*	0.0158
Female	−0.0108	0.0146	0.0100	0.0158	0.0006	0.0154
Some college	−0.0289*	0.0118	−0.0321*	0.0119	−0.0298*	0.0117
Associate's degree	−0.0932*	0.0194	−0.0955*	0.0193	−0.0918*	0.0193
Bachelor's degree	−0.1454*	0.0215	−0.1546*	0.0206	−0.1559*	0.0202
Single	−0.0790*	0.0144	−0.0748*	0.0163	−0.0505*	0.0148
Divorced	0.1580*	0.0310	0.1312*	0.0326	0.1384*	0.0324
One child	0.0141	0.0336	0.0240	0.0343	0.0195	0.0337
Two children	0.0452	0.0372	0.0608	0.0384	0.0552	0.0377
Three or more children	0.0982*	0.0392	0.0981*	0.0396	0.0976*	0.0391
Child less than age five	0.0132	0.0317	0.0155	0.0318	0.0291	0.0317
Family income per month						
$1–1,000	−0.0556*	0.0237	−0.0505*	0.0242		
$1,001–2,000	−0.0313*	0.0136	−0.0285	0.0145		
$3,001–4,000	−0.1003*	0.0173	−0.0878*	0.0192		
$4,001–5,000	−0.1317*	0.0231	−0.1199*	0.0255		
$5,001 and above	−0.1560*	0.0283	−0.1487*	0.0294		
Deployed longer than 30 days			0.0282*	0.0113	0.0237*	0.0112
Live on-base			−0.0171	0.0123	−0.0055	0.0117
Serve on ship			−0.0010	0.0210	0.0000	0.0207
Spouse in military			−0.0619*	0.0239	−0.0805*	0.0215
Assigned to base in United States			0.1012*	0.0127	0.1019*	0.0125
Spouse has full-time civilian job			−0.0215	0.0165		
Regularly exceed 50-hour workweek			0.0267*	0.0113	0.0252*	0.0112
Holds civilian job			0.0890*	0.0172		
Less than four years in military			0.0557*	0.0145	0.0676*	0.0139
Separated from spouse and child(ren)			0.1089*	0.0327	0.1175*	0.0327
Separated from spouse only			0.0629	0.0340	0.0701*	0.0340

Table 4.2—continued

Characteristic	Without Military Characteristics		With Military Characteristics		Excluding Suspect Variables	
	dF/dX	Standard Error	dF/dX	Standard Error	dF/dX	Standard Error
Separated from child(ren) only			0.1068*	0.0383	0.1054*	0.0380
Navy	−0.0834*	0.0123	−0.0894*	0.0159	−0.0871*	0.0157
Marine Corps	−0.0386*	0.0151	−0.0492*	0.0149	−0.0474*	0.0148
Air Force	−0.1411*	0.0121	−0.1275*	0.0131	−0.1242*	0.0131

NOTE: The estimated effects (dF/dX) correspond to changes in the probability relative to the excluded reference category for discrete variables and the derivative of the probability for continuous variables. Entries with asterisks are associated with coefficients that are significant at the $\alpha = 0.05$ confidence level.

hand, a member may take a second job *because* of bill-paying problems. Although we cannot discern the true direction of these effects, these variables are worth exploring. In either case, the results from the third model show that the remaining coefficients are relatively stable with reference to the second regression results.

Key variables can be loosely organized into five categories: experience and education, income, marital status, family separation, and military characteristics. Unless otherwise noted, coefficient values refer to the results from the third model.

Experience and Education

Previously, we could not distinguish much difference between the financial condition of members with four or fewer years of service and members with more experience. Because we hypothesize that members with fewer years of service were more susceptible to financial difficulties, one possible reason we did not find substantial differences may be that we did not winnow out factors that were correlated with less experience and a more positive financial condition—e.g., not being married or not having any dependent children. Including such variables in the regression model allows us to separate the variability in finances correlated with these factors.

The results in Table 4.2 show that the rate of serious problems in paying bills is 6.8 percentage points higher for members with four or fewer years of service than for members with more military experience. This supports our hypothesis that less-experienced military members are more prone to having financial problems.

The coefficient values for education and age also support our hypothesis that having more experience and hence knowledge is correlated with having fewer financial problems. Members having a two-year college degree are 9.2 percentage points less likely to have reported having financial problems than are members with only a high school (or less) education. A member with a four-year college degree is even less likely with a 15.6 percentage point drop in probability. The older, and presumably the more knowledgeable, the member, the less likely he or she is to have a financial problem. Note the subtle difference between the interpretation for the age and length of military service. Although both serve as proxies for experience, the former refers to general adult maturity while the latter refers to the nuances of the military experience that might affect finances.

Income

We investigate the possibility that members who earn less are more likely to have difficulty in staying within their budget and therefore more likely to have problems paying their bills.

The results of the second regression (with military characteristics) suggest financial problems vary little among members with monthly income in the $1,000 to $3,000 range, where 80 percent of members fall. Members at both ends of the income range have lower occurrences of bill problems. Low-income members with monthly family incomes of $1,000 or less have a 5 percentage point lower tendency to have bill problems than those in the $1,000 to $3,000 range, while high-income members with monthly incomes greater than $3,000 have 9 to 16 percentage points lower tendencies. These results parallel that of the combined military and civilian model in Chapter Three.

Depending on the service, 11 to 16 percent of members hold civilian jobs in addition to their full-time military position. We include this variable in the second regression model to explore the reasons behind their deciding to take a second job.

The coefficient for the second job variable is significant and positive. On the surface, it suggests that the typical member holding a civilian job is 8.9 percentage points more likely to report having financial difficulties than a member without a second job. But caution is warranted in interpreting this variable's coefficient. It is unlikely that having a second job per se increases a member's probability of having financial problems. Rather, members in financial trouble may decide to take another job to help pay their mounting bills. The positive coefficient likely reflects this predicament. The fact that the coefficient is positive weakens the other possible explanation in which members take a second job not to help pay necessary bills but to help pay for "luxuries," such as vacations or new household goods.

The model also adjusts for whether the military spouse is working full time. The results show that a civilian spouse who works full time has no significant effect on whether the family has financial problems. Earnings from a second job increase family income, but family expenses and spending may also increase. The results indicate that on net these families have neither more nor fewer financial problems than families without working spouses.

Marital Status and Children

Although the enlisted military population is young compared with the civilian population, more than half of members are either married or divorced. In addition, more than 13 percent of members have three or more children. This tendency of members to marry young and have children may have serious financial ramifications.

For example, the rate of serious bill problems is 5 percentage points lower for single members than for married members. Bill problems are also 14 percentage points higher for divorced members than for married members. These higher rates of problems among members who are married or divorced may reflect the substantial and perhaps unprepared extra burden of responsibilities that they incur in getting married and having to provide for other people.

Figure 4.3 reports the predicted probabilities for financial problems among members with different marital and dependent status. Other things being equal, about 23 percent of single, never-married mem-

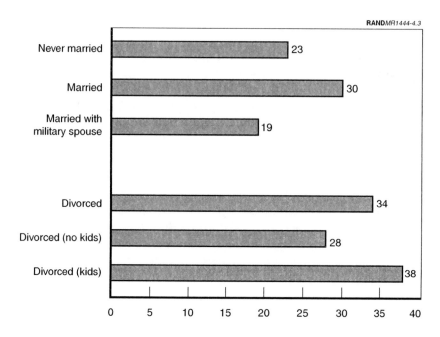

Figure 4.3—Predicted Percentage with Serious Bill Problems by Marital and Dependent Status

bers have had a serious problem paying bills in the past year. Members with a military spouse have a 4 percentage point lower probability of having bill problems than do single, nondivorced members. As Figure 4.3 shows, the probability of bill problems is substantially higher for other married members and for divorced members than for single members.

Family Separation

Because military work commitments often require frequent moves, members may decide to move without their spouse or children to mitigate hardships stemming from moving. Of the *entire* military population, 10 percent had indicated that they were separated from a spouse or child(ren) or both. If we consider only the relevant sub-population, i.e., those with dependents, this number increases to 16 percent.

There may be many varying reasons for family separation stemming from permanent change of station (PCS) moves. For example, if a child is in high school, a family may consider letting the child finish at the same school rather than force him or her to adjust to a new high school. Thus, the mother or father would stay with the child, and the member would move to his or her new assignment. Because this separation entails providing for two homes, financial hardships may be incurred. The study investigates whether varying forms of family separation stemming from change of duty station indicate differing propensities for financial difficulties.

We break down family separation stemming from PCS into three categories: separated from spouse and child(ren), separated from spouse only, separated from child(ren) only. For privacy reasons, the ADP data did not distinguish members of the family from whom the members were separated. Therefore, certain assumptions were made:

- If the member were married with children, the member was separated from both the spouse and children.

- If the member had children but was not married (i.e., single or divorced), the member was separated from only the children.

- If the member was married with no children, the member was separated only from his or her spouse.

The results indicate that any type of family separation increases the likelihood of having financial problems by 7 to 12 percentage points compared with comparable members living with their family members. The results correspond with the theory that family separation adds to financial strain because the same budget needs to meet not only additional housing costs but also transportation and contact costs—e.g., airplane tickets, long-distance telephone bills.

Members separated from their families (with children) or only from their children pose an increase of approximately 11 percentage points greater likelihood of having financial difficulties. Those separated from only their spouse still show (though to a lesser extent) a greater likelihood of having financial problems. Most likely, spouse separation stems from the spouse staying for job-related commitments. The extra job mitigates the extra expenses incurred. However, note that the differences in probability of financial strain across types of family separation are not statistically significant.

Military Characteristics

Unique attributes of military life may increase or decrease propensities for having financial difficulties. For example, it was hypothesized that members who live on base or served on ships were less likely to have financial problems. This is because members who live on base have all the basic needs—e.g., housing and food—prepaid. Thus, these members only need to budget for such optional amenities as telephone, cable, car, and entertainment. Members who serve on a ship also have their shelter and food provided. In addition, because they spend much of their time at sea, they have less opportunity to spend their money on "luxury" items.

However, the coefficients for on-ship and on-base living were found to be insignificant. This suggests that living on base versus off base and serving on board a ship versus serving on shore makes no discernible difference in the probability of financial difficulties. Even when we isolated the sample to include only Navy members, being stationed on a ship had no effect on financial status.

Unlike most civilians, military members are considered to be on call 24 hours a day, seven days a week. Nearly 50 percent of members reported regularly working more than 50 hours a week. Only 10 percent of these members also reported holding a civilian job. Thus, at least 90 percent of these members work more than 50 hours a week exclusively to satisfy their military duties. Those who did report regularly working more than 50 hours a week were 3 percentage points more likely to have financial problems. Because military members are salaried, the longer hours worked cannot be interpreted as voluntary work for extra pay. Thus, members are not being compensated for the extra time and may have difficulty in managing their time between work and household organization, including paying the bills.

Another unique element of the military is deployments. They are a common occurrence that may entail being away from permanent duty station for a maximum of six months at a time.

As Figure 4.4 depicts, certain services see more time away from their permanent duty stations than others. For example, extremely long total deployed times, greater than seven months, are relatively rare in the Air Force. In contrast, 30 percent of Navy members were deployed more than seven months out of the year.

We hypothesize that being away from home may increase the difficulty in managing bills and paying them on time.[1] Married members

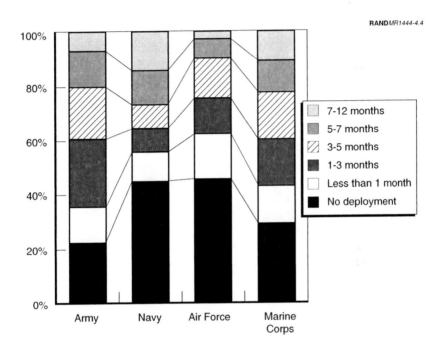

Figure 4.4—Time Deployed in Past 12 Months by Military Service

---

[1]Military members also receive special pay for deployments (Hosek and Totten, 1998). The size of the payment depends on the type and length of deployment. For example, members involuntarily separated from their family members for at least 30 consecutive days receive $105 per month in family separation allowance. If the deployment is in a hostile area, then the member receives an additional $150 per month. The survey does not distinguish among different types of deployments and does not separate deployment-related income from other sources of income. The results in the text reflect the fact that bill-paying problems of deployed members exceed those of non-deployed members, despite the extra deployment pay earned by deployed members.

sometimes have difficulty coordinating their spending because they communicate less frequently than when the member is at home. Moreover, frequent short-term deployments in a year may be even more disruptive than one long-term deployment. Unfortunately, the 1999 survey only provided the total amount of time deployed and the numbers of times deployed; it did not offer information of each deployment and its corresponding lengths. Hence, although we could have calculated the averaged length of deployment, we could not distinguish between multiple short-term deployments and one single long-term deployment. Consequently, a binary variable indicating that a member had been deployed for more than a total of one month was used. Though clumping may have masked the variations among lengths of deployments, the resulting coefficient does indicate that members who were deployed for a total length greater than one month are 2.4 percentage points more likely to have financial problems than nondeployed members.

Because of the varying distribution of deployment times among military services, additional models exploring deployment effects particular to each service were conducted. These models include all the controlling variables listed in Table 4.2. The only difference is that the regression was performed for each service separately. Results indicate that Army and Marine Corps members who were deployed longer than one month are approximately 6 percentage points more likely to have financial problems. However, members in the Navy and Air Force who were deployed longer than one month are no more likely to have financial problems.

Finally, the results in Table 4.2 show that significant differences in financial problems arise across the service branches after controlling for demographics, family situation, and military environment. Figure 4.5 shows that the Army and Marine Corps have a somewhat higher incidence of problems than the Navy and Air Force. Some might argue that the Army has more problems than the Air Force because the Army members are younger, less well educated, and more likely to be deployed than are airmen. Our statistical results suggest that even if we looked at comparable members of the Army and Air Force, however, the probability of an Army member having financial problems in the past year is 14 percentage points higher than that for a comparable airman.

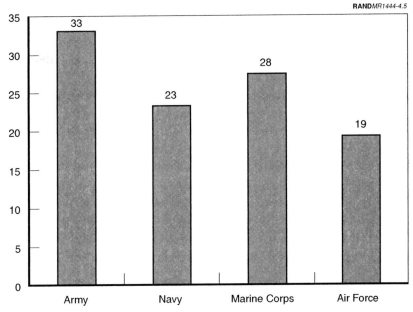

RAND*MR1444-4.5*

Figure 4.5—Percentage of Individuals with Serious Problems Paying Bills
by Service Branch (Adjusted for Demographic, Family Factors, and
Military Environment)

Why does the incidence of financial problems for comparable members differ across services? Several explanations are possible. First, the Navy and Air Force may be more effective in teaching financial skills than are the other services. This explanation seems unlikely to us because the curriculum and courses are similar across the service branches. Second, the Air Force may have fewer problems than other services because of its career orientation. This career outlook may mean that young airmen are more conscientious about avoiding financial pitfalls that might hurt their career prospects than are junior members of other services with little interest in a military career. Similarly, the Air Force has a larger pool of senior enlisted and officer personnel than the other services who may serve as mentors for junior airmen. Finally, of course, a variety of unmeasured factors may partially explain service-related differences in bill-paying problems. For example, Army and Marine Corps bases are generally quite large and in remote areas, meaning that competition among local merchants may be limited and opportunities for spouse employment (especially suitable employment for the spouse's training and experience) are few (Wardynski, 2000). In contrast, Navy members generally live in urban port cities with diverse markets and opportunities. Air bases are often remote, but the military population in these areas in generally a smaller share of the local economy than is the case for Army or Marine Corps bases.

Chapter Five

SUMMARY AND CONCLUSIONS

This study examines the personal financial conditions of junior enlisted members in the Army, Navy, Air Force, and Marines. It compares the prevalence and severity of financial problems between the civilian and military population and examines various situations unique to the military that may affect members' economic well-being.

The results indicate that military members are much more likely to experience financial pressure from creditors in the previous year than are civilians. After controlling for demographic and other differences between the military and civilian populations, we estimate that only 10 percent of comparable civilians have creditor problems in contrast to 23 and 18 percent of military members in 1997 and 1999, respectively.

We also examine a broader class of serious problems in paying bills (e.g., pressured by creditor to pay bills, had utilities shut off, pawned or sold valuables to pay bills, fell behind in rent or mortgage, had belongings repossessed, or filed for bankruptcy). After adjusting for varying characteristics of military members and civilians, we find that military members have a much higher probability of bill problems than do civilians, 27 versus 18 percent, respectively.

Demographic and family factors affect military members and civilians in the same way. Problems with creditor pressure and paying bills both decline somewhat with age and with increased education. Blacks have more problems than both Hispanics and white non-Hispanics.

The results suggest that recent military efforts to reduce financial problems have been met with modest success. There was some reduction in the proportion of military members that reported pressure from creditors (from 23 percent in 1997 to 18 percent in 1999), but the incidence of serious bill problems remained at 27 percent over this two-year period. By both measures, the extent of financial problems among military members remains an order of magnitude higher than for comparable civilians.

In our earlier study (Tiemeyer et al., 1999), we proposed that new financial training should be phased in, so the effectiveness of the programs could be systematically evaluated. However, the new programs were hastily adapted; consequently, no meaningful benchmarking for the effectiveness of class enrollment or course curriculum occurred. Our results show that the extent of problems has shown no strong tendency for convergence to the civilian norm. Without a careful evaluation of the classroom programs, however, we cannot evaluate the effectiveness of specific programs or recommend how they should be modified.

Deployments, long hours, and family separations are common in the military, and these factors all contribute to financial problems of members. DoD should investigate whether some personnel-support programs could help with these problems. For example, improved Internet and telephone access with families during deployments might reduce some financial coordination problems between members and their families. In addition, reassignment patterns could be modified to ease the likelihood of family separations and their implications on family finances. Of course, the implication of these types of policies on family finances is just one component of their value to members that must be weighed against the cost implications of these policies.

A key insight of this study is that two key factors are unrelated to financial distress for members. First, financial problems are not more common for members in off-base housing than for those living on base. There are various reasons to expand or contract the stock of on-base housing, but our result suggests that these policies will have little effect on the extent of members' financial problems. Second, financial problems are not related to family income. Higher military pay would improve the well-being of members and their families, but our results suggest that the pay increase would do little to reduce the extent of financial problems among members. This finding suggests that financial problems are shaped by spending patterns and management skills rather than by income itself.

We would encourage DoD and the military services to implement a systematic evaluation of financial management programs. This evaluation would vary course offerings among members, test member financial skills before and after each type of training, and assess financial problems of members over time. This approach would identify which types of training are most effective and offer a clear path for how to reduce financial problems.

Our base visits did suggest two relatively untapped approaches that merit serious attention. First, unit officials provide considerable "hands-on" financial advice to young members, but these efforts are not well integrated with formal financial management classes. Too often, it appeared that unit leaders saw their efforts as alternatives to formal instruction and referred members to the formal programs as a last resort. We suspect that the personnel support managers could do a better outreach effort to advise unit leaders on how to "informally" help members. Second, the services should endeavor to reduce the stigma associated with financial counseling. Members are reluctant to use available services because they believe that they will be punished by the military for their financial situation. Similarly, some unit leaders are reluctant to recommend formal counseling for a member because they believe that a record of counseling will jeopardize the member's military future. One-on-one counseling could help members build a budget or arrange a consolidation loan, but the stigma of using the counseling services discourages members from taking advantage of these services.

BIBLIOGRAPHY

Asch, Beth J., and James R. Hosek, *Military Compensation: Trends and Policy Options*, Santa Monica, Calif.: RAND, DB-273-OSD, 1999.

Bray, Robert M., Rebecca P. Sanchez, Miriam L. Ornstein, Danielle Lentine, Amy A. Vincus, Tracy U. Baird, June A. Walker, Sara C. Wheeless, L. Lynn Guess, Larry A. Kroutil, and Vincent G. Iannacchione, *1998 Department of Defense Survey of Health Related Behaviors Among Military Personnel*, Research Triangle Park, N.C.: Research Triangle Institute, 1999.

Buddin, Richard, *Building a Personnel Support Agenda: Goals, Analysis Framework, and Data Requirements*, Santa Monica, Calif.: RAND, MR-916-OSD, 1998.

Buddin, Richard, Carole Roan Gresenz, Susan D. Hosek, Marc Elliot, and Jennifer Hawes-Dawson, *An Evaluation of Housing Options for Military Families*, Santa Monica, Calif.: RAND, MR-1020-OSD, 1999.

Hosek, James R., and Mark Totten, *Does Perstempo Hurt Reenlistment? The Effect of Long or Hostile Perstempo on Reenlistment*, Santa Monica, Calif.: RAND, MR-990-OSD, 1998.

Kennickell, Arthur B., Martha Starr-McCluer, and Brian J. Surette, "Recent Changes in U.S. Family Finances: Results from the 1998 Survey of Consumer Finances," *Federal Reserve Bulletin*, January 2000.

Luther, Raminder K., E. Thomas Garman, Irene E. Leech, Larry Griffitt, and Timothy Gilroy, *Scope and Impact of Personal Financial Management Difficulties of Service Members on the Department of the Navy*, Scranton, Pa.: Military Family Institute, Report 97-1, 1997.

Report of the Congressional Commission on Servicemembers and Veterans Transition Assistance, January 1999.

Segal, Mady Wechsler, and Jesse J. Harris, "What We Know About Military Families," Alexandria, Va.: U.S. Army Research Institute for the Behavioral and Social Sciences, 1993.

Stone, Paul, "DoD Offers Dollars and Sense Guide to Managing Your Finances," American Forces Press Service, 1998.

Tiemeyer, Peter, Casey Wardynski, and Richard Buddin, *Financial Management Problems Among Enlisted Personnel*, Santa Monica, Calif.: RAND, DB-241-OSD, 1999.

Wardynski, Casey, *Military Compensation in the Age of Two-Income Households: Adding Spouses' Earnings to the Compensation Policy Mix*, Santa Monica, Calif.: RAND, RGSD-154, 2000.

Wright, Laverne C., Kristen Williams, and Elizabeth J. Willis, *1999 Survey of Active Duty Personnel: Administration, Datasets, and Codebook*, Arlington, Va.: Defense Manpower Data Center, DMDC Report No. 2000-005, December 2000.